What if?

a book about recycling

Mick Manning and
Brita Granström

W
FRANKLIN WATTS
LONDON • SYDNEY

All sorts of things could happen to a thrown-away bottle. What if, it became a trap for small animals?

Thrown-away glass bottles can become traps.
If the bottles break they can cut people and animals.

3

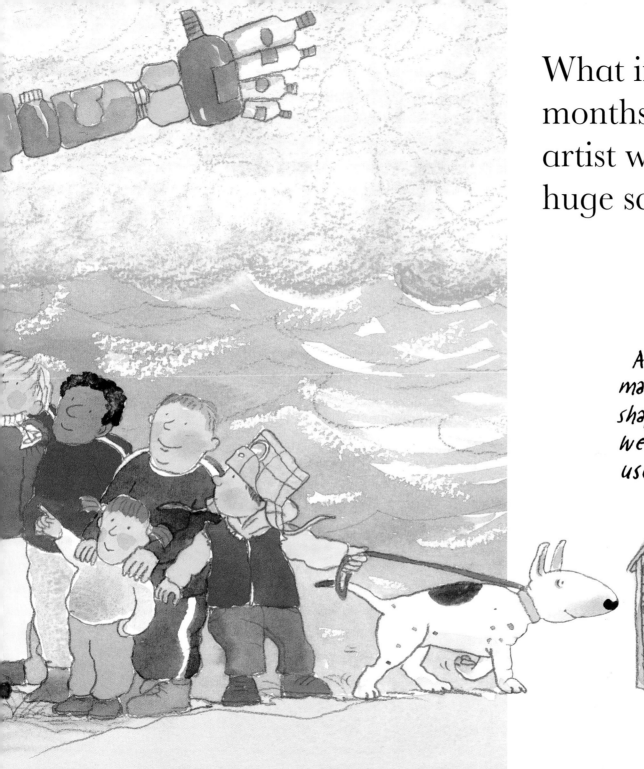

What if, it was found a few months later by a famous artist who made it part of a huge sculpture?

A German company once made beer bottles in the shape of bricks. When they were empty people could use them to build houses.

What if, the bottle broke? It would take hundreds of sea storms to wear the finger-slicing broken glass into smooth pebbles.

Wind and water wear away cliffs and rocks and reshape them.

cliff

wind and waves

stones

sand

What if, you found the bottle and put a message inside, with a toy boat to stand guard. Then you threw it into the sea?

Long ago, a message in a bottle was the only way people who lived on far-away islands like St.Kilda could contact the mainland.

You should not throw litter into the sea or anywhere else!

9

What if, the tide carried your bobbing bottle into a whirlpool and it got dragged deep down to the bottom of the sea?

Shipwrecks and other litter on the sea bed can be salvaged and recycled.

10

What if, the bottle finally bobbed back up to the surface and sharks poked it curiously with their snouts as it floated on the waves?

Sometimes sharks swallow sharp metal, and turtles will swallow plastic bags thinking they are jellyfish - this can kill them.

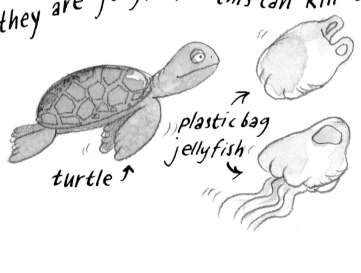

turtle ↑

plastic bag

jellyfish

What if, after weeks of drifting across the ocean, your bottle was washed up on a far-away beach?

Litter can travel long distances in the sea. The rubbish on beaches comes from all over the world—

coconut

old toy from somewhere

fishing float

old gold coin from a shipwreck

swedish hairspray

old dummy

Russian log book

What if, a beachguard, cleaning up the beach, found the bottle and tossed it into a skip?

Many things can be recycled instead of thrown away, this includes...

cardboard

cans

newspaper

tyres and plastic bottles.

glass

batteries

What if, the skip was taken by lorry to a recycling plant, where the bottles got sorted and put onto a conveyor belt?

GREEN   WHITE   BROWN

Collection points for bottles are sometimes called 'bottle banks'.

19

What if, after your bottle got washed it continued along the conveyor with thousands of other bottles...to be smashed into smithereens?

cleaned

used bottles collected

moulded into a new bottle

cleaned

magnet takes away metal tops

melted in a furnace

crushed into cullet

magnet

glass crusher

21

What if, the crushed bottles were sent to a furnace to be melted down into a red hot soup of liquid glass.

Recycled glass can be used for making new bottles, paint for road markings and fibre glass.

Fibre glass is used for making cars, planes and many other things.

Wait a minute!
What if, just before
your bottle was
crushed and melted
down someone
spotted your
message?

some glass bottles, mostly green
ones contain quite a lot of
recycled glass already.

24

25

What if, some day you got a parcel in the post from a far-away country? And when you opened it you found a shiny, new, green bottle with your boat, and a message inside!

Hi Kid!
Recycle your own
rubbish next time!

Love
from Joe
(and everyone at the
bottle factory)

27

Many everyday things can be recycled instead of thrown away. Perhaps there are some collection sites near you?

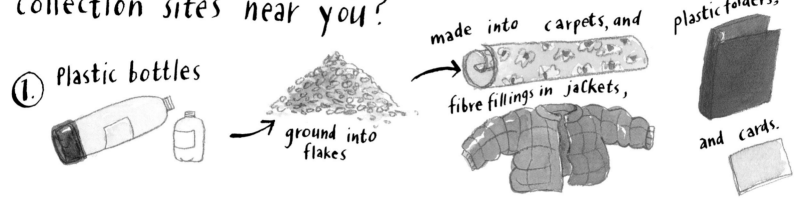

① Plastic bottles → ground into flakes → made into carpets, and fibre fillings in jackets, plastic folders, and cards.

② Aluminium cans → squashed and ground into flakes → melted into shiny new aluminium sheets... to make new cans!

③ Other metal cans → squashed and melted in a steel factory → made into metal bars, pipes and concrete reinforcing

④ Glass
crushed into powder
melted and made into new bottles
or made into paint for road markings and road signs
or made into fibreglass

⑤ Tyres
melted down
made into rubber mats
and running tracks.

⑥ Newspapers
baled up
pulped into liquid paper at papermill
made into phonebooks and new newspapers.

Helpful words

Cullet is the proper name for crushed glass before it gets melted.

Energy is the power to make things work. We need energy for light and heat, to work machines in factories, and to run vehicles like cars, trucks and planes. A lot of energy is used making glass bottles!

Furnace is like a very, very hot oven which melts down glass or metal into liquid.

Pollution is the poison and mess in the air, land and sea created by our rubbish. Pollution can kill plants and animals, it can harm us too.

Re-use is when something is used again instead of being thrown away – like mixing paint in an old jam jar or re-using an envelope to save paper.

Recycle is when you make something new from unwanted, empty or thrown-away things. For example, empty bottles can be melted down and made into new ones.

Resources are the Earth's raw materials such as wood, coal, rock and oil that we use to make everyday things. We must use Earth's resources carefully. What would we do without them?

Rubbish People make so much rubbish; where does it all go when you put it in the bin? Some gets burned which causes pollution, but most goes to your local waste disposal site. These are often dirty, dangerous places with rats and germs. Many countries have started to sort and recycle as much of their rubbish as they can.

What can you do to help?

To help save the Earth's resources and prevent pollution you could try re-using things such as envelopes to save paper, and plastic bags which can be used over and over again. Ask your family and school to recycle as much rubbish as possible. There are local collection points for all sorts of glass, paper, cartons, cans and plastic bottles.

For Steve Robinson

This edition 2004

First published by Franklin Watts,
338 Euston Road, London, NW1 3BH

Franklin Watts Australia
Level 17/207 Kent Street, Sydney, NSW 2000

Text and illustrations © 1998 Mick Manning and Brita Granström
Notes and activities © 2004 Franklin Watts

The illustrations in the book were made by Brita and Mick
Find out more about Mick and Brita on www.mickandbrita.com

Series editor: Paula Borton
Art director: Robert Walster

Thanks to British Glass and Shelley Vandenberg at UBC Waste
Management

Printed in Singapore

A CIP catalogue record is available from the British Library.

Dewey Classification 363.72

ISBN 978 0 7496 5692 8

Franklin Watts is a division of Hachette Children's Books,
an Hachette Livre UK company.